Greening

Poetry of the Spring

Mandy Whyman

Lavender Button Books

Cover image : PICSAR – Unsplash

To my daughters

there is wonder all around us, even when the world seems bleak.

CONTENTS

Fabric

The patchworked quilt of England's Spring,

When ploughed land lies in pinstripes

Beside the cottoned yellow of the rape.

Where gingham green

Lies between

The over-stitched lines of hedgerows

And wild cherry burst silk white

Beneath a voile sky.

Greening

Then:

Like a watercolour wash,

Like the stippling of a pen

The canvas colours over

And life begins again.

Hard worn roadside edges

Beaten to bleak and mud,

Hoist hopeful pennants of glassy green,

Burst in shields of dandelions.

Hedgerows puff: fill in, fill out,

Ripen in their readiness.

Primrose, crocus, celandine

Blush verges into bunting.

Trees tuck and dart in verdant folds,

Sway in silks of emerald, peridot and jade.

Shy cherry blossom flushes

Against the last of blackthorn snow…

Greening and gathering.

The world cascades to colour,

Suddenly, like birdsong –

Spring!

Life

I believe in life,

The tenacity of it all,

The miracles of seasons:

The fallen tree that reaches,

Green and growing skywards,

New growth.

The frogs that return each year

To the ponds where they were spawned.

The swallows that cross deserts

To follow Summer's hand.

I believe in life

That bursts quiet in small things:

The brambles that clamber, reclaim

Gullies where trains once ran.

The dandelions that flower

Despite the gravelled yards,

The way that celandine and lambs cress

Are seeded by the wind.

That a single season is all it takes

For poppies, bright and red, to push through trampled earth

Of building sites on flattened fields.

How an untended corner

Gathers life like stardust

In clover and daisies and elder

Bringing woodlice, spiders, aphids, ladybirds, butterflies

And robins and blackbirds and wrens

And little pipistrelle bats.

Until life bubbles and bursts

In an overflow of everything…

I believe in life.

In the tenacity of it all.

The way it will not be contained

Despite our mowing and our tweaking

Our fake grass and garden walls.

If I Were

If I were a tree

I'd live

With arms thrown back and face to the sun.

I would dream in the march of seasons

Feel the beat of a heart

Rooted deep in the pulse of the Earth,

Grafted to arteries, nerves.

I would sing the very air –

Reach the wind, the storm, the satin rain.

Cradle a whole existence

Of feathers and small things and life.

Be.

I would not be afraid to die –

Because the felling of me

Would be the end

Of everything.

The Arrival

The frogs arrive in the night.

In the morning they hang:

Resting athletes, long legs dangling,

A gang with bulbous eyes

Just above the water line.

They burp out their arrival –

First four, then eight

And through the week, they multiply,

Until a colony

Fills the corner of the pond.

The water reverberates

With a low rumbling chorus

Of ardent love-song.

They hiccup into silence

And dash for pond-deep cover

At the fall of my shadow.

Silence.

If I watch still, for long enough,

The eyes lift above the water line

And they hang like bar-room regulars.

Their burping song begins again.

I watch -

They watch me back.

March Field

The field is ploughed,

Roughed with last year's crop detritus.

Waiting.

Just the path runs straight and smooth,

Worn down by daily dog-walking shoes

Across a wasteland:

Mud field beneath a sullen sky.

And still

Magic beats here,

Where the buzz of the motorway grows dim,

Where the air tumbles with the trilling thrill

Of the skylark's song

Rolling in from somewhere invisible,

Like the soundtrack to a miracle:

The Spring that lies just beyond imagining.

Dreaming, stirring, embryonic,

Deep in the sleeping, warming, muddied

March field.

Pond courtship

It's a strange, web-footed dance
In the shallows of the pond –
All dart and drift
And hanging about,
Goggled eyes above water,
White-throated vocals bubbling and blurting
Come-hither burps…

The undignified scattering,
Clambering, slipping, wrapping.
Perhaps a lucky-chance clasping
In head to chin leathery embrace.
A dance of endurance,
Determined dodging and diving.
Something almost tender…

Until, In the morning,

The bubbling pearlescent evidence

Of a pond courtship.

Daffodils

Yellow frilled eyelashes flutter
With the bend of sinewy stems:
Seducers, imposters,
Promising the sun.

They crowd in yellow bonnets,
Wind-blown and faking cheeriness,
Huddled in groups
Like squabbling schoolgirls.

The pale fragility is a lie –
That frilled finery is teflon-tough
Against the blasts of March.
In the still-warming earth
Their shallot-shaped hearts
Hold poison.

Grandma used to say:

The good weather only comes,

When the daffodils die away.

Last Year

Last year
We walked these paths –
The routes through sold-off farmer's fields
With wooden gates and old cow troughs
And camomile like runs of lace.

This year
The paths are fenced
And signs make clear
No walking or wondering is wanted here.
They've dug the sewers, tarred the land,
Raised the ugly houses that promise profits.

Alone,
A fenced oak
Stands in gaunt submission.

While the thud of the pile-driver

Silences the hedgerows,

Subdues the undulations,

Drives nails into the heart

Of the place where the camomile once grew.

Break in the Rain

The sun breaks suddenly through the rain,

Silvering the edges of the looming cloud sails –

Battlements of purple against the bright

That dazzles the drenched earth,

Polishing puddles into mirrors

And jewelling the new spring growth

Into jade, emerald, malachite.

Hanging diamonds from every quivering leaf,

Glittering glassed grass on field edges…

A blackbird watches from the hedgerow,

Its eye yellow-rimmed in light.

The high, lilting syllables of a robin's bubbling song

Courses into the new-stilled air.

Under the sudden sun, with the rain-wet ground

Be-jewelled,

The whole world is re-made:

Washed bright;

New.

Spring in the Garden

Spring comes to the garden

Before the weather turns warm,

When the portly pigeon parades himself

Along the fence's edge,

All puff and bow and strutting -

And swift, side-eyed rejection.

Spring comes to the garden

In the dark-darting blackbird's song

That conjures light to days

Grown minutely longer,

Trilled awake in the piping cadences

Of Spring's first bird.

Spring comes to the garden

In a creeping greening,

The slow unfurling of tight-twirled buds'

Tender leaf-wing openings

Spreading like hearts

To the touch of a warming sun.

Spring comes.

Yellow

Yellow
Like butter
And buttoned sunlight
Dapples March's edges
In optimism.

Daffodils
Dressed in flaxen lace
Bob in every flower box
And along the garden edges
Coy with Springtime come-hitherness.

Forsythia
All flamenco and frills
Bursts froths of canary feathers,
Neon against the blackthorn, cherry –
Long-legged dancers of the verges.

Dandelions

Creep into lawns and gaps

And crowd the front doorstep,

Open dark-rimmed eyes

Wide into a plate of golden rays –

Bright small suns of Spring.

Yellow.

Song

In the small hours of the morning

The blackbird sings to me,

In clarity so pure

That all the universe seems poised,

Caught in the whistle and the trill

So completely

That every fibre of the world trembles awake.

The dawn stretches, soft-limbed,

Piped by the blackbird's song

And the notes become solidified

Into rays that reach golden

To gild the chimney pots.

Promise and hope,

Light and love

Heart-words too wide to be spoken –

Fluted clear and sure into daybreak –

The world in the blackbird's song.

The Way

I don't want to walk today.

Thoughts hang heavy 'round my heart,

Cloud my head, turn legs to lead.

But I do –

Urged on by the dog's eager tug,

Out into the silent morning.

It's a good path:

Red earth worn hard

Beneath so many walkers' shoes

And it rings back to my heartbeat

      On, on, on

To where the break in the fields

Divides the land

And the rape crop begins to show

      On, on, on

Past hedgerows

Where robins wake and sparrows squabble.

The faraway traffic hums, somnambulant

While other lives take up other beats.

Here the steady thud of the way

Leads me

     On, on, on

Led by the dog and the pull of my heart

To where a brook lilts silver

And the stalks of last year's crop show like bones

     On, on, on

To where the skylarks rill and dip.

Where the land grows wide to meet the sky.

Where,

Weightless

My heart falls empty open

And the wind breathes through me

So that everything and all

Is the land, the song and the pull of air…

The dog grins in wide-mouthed knowing,

Tongue-lolling joy,

Streaks away down the beckoning path,

On, on, on.

April Showers

April showers

Monsoon into days.

The world drips dreary –

Edges washed into blurs

That take on a pallor

Not in keeping with spring.

How strange to see

Bedraggled pigeons congregate,

Puff and preen in flat roof puddles.

Pom-pommed sparrows

Bustle about the dripping hedge edges,

Their gossip loud against the rain.

Rooks parade the lawn

Black and slick with wet,

Mackintoshed inspectors – business as usual.

And the pear tree blooms so white

Against the gloom,

And battered dandelions

Stand steadfast in their sun-mimicry –

Beacons

Against the astonishing green of it all.

It is me who is cowed,

Put to shame by the rain…

Outside,

Spring marches on

Undeterred and undefeated.

Into the Woods

And so… into the woods –

Into the arms of trees

That dapple the summering sky

And whisper rumours of seasons gone by.

Into the woods on a trail worn hard

Beneath a sprawling, gathering green,

Where the world is muted,

Leaf-litter muffled,

Where silence hums the songs of small birds.

The outside world hazes over, disappears,

The track unravels the years.

I could be anyone, any time,

Stepping this path well worn

With memories and echoes

Into the long silence that beckons

The way

Into the woods.

Stain

All week it is there

Turning more stain than creature.

Small and smashed

Just the waving plume of brush

(Like a funeral flag)

To tell the young it once was.

There is something poignant

In the way it lies,

Nose forward

Headed for the summer,

As if it may have lived.

A newspaper reports

A `near catastrophic' decline in red foxes.

The stain rusts to nothing,

The brush falling and fading

Like the last of the evening's cloud.

The Wall

It's not Time that eats at the boundary wall,

Built high and bricked and coppice-stoned –

It's the winter that has gnawed the clay,

The sun that has chipped it, crumbling it away.

It's the old wisteria that has unsettled the seams,

Reaching grey fingers to where binding used to be.

It is the roots of the cherry tree that displace the
footings,

The aubrieta that has seeded on the high ledge,

And tumbles down in purple tears.

It is the birds that peck at moss,

Loosen up the binding,

Where spiders build their funnel webs

And the rain silvers in like mercury.

The boundary blurs for the wall –

The clay crumbles and coppice stones that once were grand,

Are unseated by the seasons,

By the green embrace of Life.

Heron

The heron comes in like a hangman,

All stealth and stilted walk:

A thief,

With hooded eye and bladed beak.

The pond edge grows silent,

Small birds cease their chatter,

Scatter

Into cover. Even the fat pigeon

Shuffles furtive away.

The heron lurks like Time –

Long-legged assassin,

Patient in the silence.

I watch, mesmerised

By the blue elegance of Death.

Until the dog's sharp bark

Lifts the heron high

On wide wings, to arc away

In the spread, sweeping V

Of some long-limbed ancient angel.

Hidden

Here, on this forgotten track,

Where no-one seems to come,

Where three-barred gates hide in hedging,

The bite of their latches long lost.

Here the rough plank fencing

Half marks the edge of fields

And the track runs black-mud thin.

Nettles crowd the edges

And stitchwort, so pretty and forgotten,

Blooms like stars.

Here the blackthorn spread their branches,

In a froth of flowered lace,

So that edges of the air touch white.

Tiny wrens dart like dark moths

And the robin flits away.

The sound of the road is muted,

By the humming of early bees,

The whispered words of trees.

This forgotten track, hidden,

Here, on the edge of Now.

Adjustment

Foil strips are spread on string

In rows across the newly seeded lawn –

A bid at an adjustment to the scene –

So metal glints and shimmies in the breeze

And wall-eyed pigeons cease their snacking

- Startle away.

Above

Corvids chortle in discussion

- Assess the situation.

Just two days of determination –

Magpies and rooks working shifts -

And shards of silver glitter from the ground

Like shiny seeds.

Fat pigeons coo and nod

-    Approve the avian adjustment.

Magpies cackle

-    Moved to other mischief.

Reflection

At the pond's edge,

In the early evening sun,

Where the marsh marigold reflects ripples

And the water sees the sky.

Midges dance like dust motes

Glittered by the light

And pond skaters sew tucks

Into the dark silken surface.

In this still afternoon,

Golden in the hum of bees

And the music of birds,

All else evaporates.

It is a sort of heaven,

Here, at the pond's edge

In the early evening sun.

Wind rider

The wind boils up into the afternoon,

Rattling at the gate

And whipping fresh-greened trees to frenzy.

A pigeon heavy-bodied braves the air –

Stalls, settles –

Tucks down with hunkered wings.

High above, bright white bellied

Against the skudding sky

A gull rolls into the blast,

Pulaski wings wide and still,

Rocked and locked in motion,

It banks and rights,

Tilts, holds the line,

Surfs the blast,

In long-winged, light-boned mastery.

The bucking roil is tamed.

The gull lifts and soars –

Wind rider.

Casting spells

I learn the names like an incantation,

A spell of the season.

The tripping ones, the children's rhyme:

Daisy, clover, buttercup and dandelion.

A gathering of enchantments from field edges:

Cow parsley, primrose, chicory, scabiousa, red campion…

Names that promise magic and charms:

Harebell, forget-me-not, dog rose and stitchwort,

Gifts from the wind and birds:

Celandine, lambs cress, poppy, aquilegia, rosebay willowherb

And tamed magic found in ordinary places:

Gaura, echinacea, lavender, marsh marigold and sweet smelling stocks.

The names trip together, mesh,

Tie buttons and lace into Spring,

Weave a spell of meadows and hedgerows and ley-lines.

Silver the heart. Gild the tongue.

Greedy Fish

I never understood
"Greedy fish",
Until I got my own.
And now they watch the pond edge,
Follow the lean of my shadow –
Eager flashes of orange
That gather and lip-smack the air
Until they are fed.
They gobble in bubbles,
Excited slapping and wrapping
Until it is gone.

Then they follow the lean of my shadow
And lip-smack for more.

Morning

Cracked moon of a morning,

Light spilling like yolk

Across the grass

To shiver dawn-soft bloomings.

The world sleeps still.

Birds weave the airways,

Still free of the traffic thrum,

Mesh like silver the silken morning,

Stitching threads of blackbird, robin, thrush -

Conjuring colour to the breaking sky.

The day

Steals on high notes,

Soft-soled,

Into a symphony of beginning.

A Bend in the Lane

The bend in the lane

Where, between high hedgerows

The last of the rooftops are lost

And cow parsley froths into daydreams.

It is easy to imagine

That this might be all.

A lane, still the same,

Lost and drifting in time,

A world made of darting robins and wrens

And gnarled trunks of aged hawthorn,

Bent and bowed to hedgerow walls.

Where all the noise is stopped

And peace casts a net in birdsong.

Where breath is.

Where hope is.

A bend in the lane

Where what is lost,

Is not.

Left Behind

Do they feel survivor's guilt?

The oak trees left behind,

The ones that made the grade and dodged the blade,

Here, on the edge of the farmer's field.

Do they feel ashamed?

The ones that stand alone in ugly new developments -

Totems to a time gone past,

Symbols of a sacrificial land.

Do they dream of summers gone,

Thick with the whispering of leaves

When oak tree forests ruled this land

And hid the likes of kings and thieves.

Do their oaken hearts bleed out

At being left behind?

While the world is flattened, paved,

And only street names remind

Of a time where the land was wild

And the world was full

Of others of their kind.

First Swallow

Late April,

And the first swallow of the season

Dips and dives over ripening rape,

Taking me back to childhood

In distant Southern lands

Where the September coming of swallows

Signalled Summer.

They lined the drooping telephone wires

Above chalk-dusty farm roads

Like paused music notes.

There seemed so many then…

Here, in a different hemisphere

The first swallow swoops,

White underbelly flashing

As he banks and rolls, sweeps past

With blue aviator cap pulled low.

A survivor of six thousand miles,

The blue-V tail, signals Victory –

A snubbing of the odds.

Here, above the yellow rape,

The dash of blue and white

Slices through the years,

Cuts a channel through my heart,

To lines of swallows like music notes.

Blue Sky

8am, and the sun's already high

In a sky cut by vapour trails

Like a wide blue cake.

Winter wheat brushes to the knee

And puddles have dried

To leave footprints like fossils.

The air seems to sleep.

Still.

And so it is

That May unfolds in growing fields

And warmth that steals

Into bird calls and verges

Dappled and dazzled

With the colours of May:

Cow parsley, buttercup, celandine,

And a sky

Like a wide blue promise.

Driving Home

Like driving through a dream:

The rain soft-gauzes the windscreen,

Blurring the borders of the way,

Mist-merging trees and sky

To soft impressionism.

A plotline, the mossed wall snakes downhill,

Greyed stones rough with stories.

Trees arch in new-hatched green,

Wild cherry blossoms confetti white

And two blackbirds dart like brushstrokes,

Disappear into edges:

Complete the Monet.

The tar runs black and sleek,

Onward like a river.

The veil of the world falls thin.

Disconnect

The sky particles into pink

And ragged clouds soften into strands

Drawn across the sky by jackdaws

Heading home.

It is a dream of forever –

We are lulled by the rhythm

Of the day that ends, that starts.

We slot into our own imaginings,

Browse pictures of perfection,

Learn to pave over gardens,

Green with plastic lawns.

We image into indifference,

Mirror-watching: forget to see, forget to care…

Somewhere

Someone posts a picture of a lapwing,

Somewhere

Someone remembers when lapwings were everywhere.

We change the thread, move on

Mow our lawns into lines,

Pluck out the imperfections,

Close the window,

Watch another nature show.

Late Afternoon

The sun is out at last

And warmth licks the late afternoon

Into velvet.

The air hangs syrup-still

Where pigeons flap and flop

In lazy arcs,

Throaty `hoo's' curling into padding for a day

Grown long and comfortable.

The lawn stretches, languid,

Confetti'd in cherry blossom.

Somewhere high and out of sight

A small aeroplane buzzes a purr.

All stillness

Is cocoon-bubbled here,

Drowsed to the hum of bees

And the scent of warm earth.

Time and all the world, pauses,

Under the dappled shade of new-greened trees,

In the warmth of a late afternoon.

Titania

Fragile.

A bee, asleep on a nettle leaf

Courted by leaves jewelled in early rain:

Titania. Dreamed in wonder

Without her Oberon –

Free of the tricks of faerie folk

And men, who stumble rough-shod

Over all that is beautiful.

She sleeps.

A small mesmer of magic.

Hope,

In a world grown weary.

Dandelion

Sun and moon in one:

Yellow-gowan, earth-nail,

Rooted to a hollow stem

And yellow-maned in dandiness –

One hundred rays stretched open,

Become a small and sudden sun

Brave against the blasts of March

And then...

A tiny miracle:

Faded florets curl to chrysalis

Armoured, sealed in twisted bracts.

Like magic, a metamorphosis,

To bloom again –

Something soft, ethereal

A moon all gossamer white

Where breath of the warming wind

Looses plumed promises -

Sends wishes into flight.

Moonlight

Daylight slips

Into deepened velvet.

A new half moon

Hangs like a silver sail

On a sea becalmed.

Sleepy jackdaws *tuc-tuc*

From nests on darkened chimney pots.

Three bats, like chasing phantoms,

Trace a figure of eight.

Its late and quiet and warm,

The air laden and lazy

With the long May day.

Shadows ink the edges of the garden,

Run little rivers of dark along the edges of the wall.

A far away owl calls –

Soft and low –

A seeker from another land.

A Robin Came to Sing to Me

A robin came to sing to me

Where I dozed on the lazy lawn

Beneath the trees.

It perched close, on the wall

And sang as if all the world

Was in this garden,

This sun,

This stippled shade.

It sang

For minutes

That bubbled to days and years

And to all the ends of every earth -

The sunshine and the dappled lawn,

When a robin came to sing to me.

Into the Storm

Driving towards the storm,

The sun behind,

And tar lit like silver,

Every green burns alight

Against a velvet sky,

Distilled and purple-deep.

Wide fields of cadmium rape roll

To greet a horizon

In startled surreal epiphany:

Every tree is etched,

Every leaf and blade line-marked,

Sun-edged,

Saturated into emotion

Too impossible to speak…

Two turbines turn

In paper-white cartwheels:

Signals against the bruise of sky.

This is what it must be to die:

The sun against our backs

And all the world ablaze

Against the storm ahead –

A rapture

And the unbearable beauty of it all.

Words

Merged into backgrounds,

I am un-made.

My atoms flow apart -

Thoughts:

An evening sky that dims.

Only words

Anchor me here –

Bind to me reality,

Tether me to birdsong,

To the leap of an open field;

To the slow warming of the sodden earth

Beneath the pink-birthing touch of sky.

Words

That catch and sketch the moment,

Breathe in the image, feed, grow:

Umbilicus to existence.

<u>One</u>

When all that is me

Is done,

Let me atomise,

Become part of the soil,

Be the dandelion, the tree.

Cling and climb with the ivy,

Be the pollen on the bee,

The dust on a butterfly's wings.

Let all my molecules

Be the breeze

That lifts the jackdaw's wing,

That ruffles at the robin's breast,

That carries seeds

High away across the fields.

Let every particle of me

Become this sun, this rain,

This wondrous, unnameable earth.

This blackbird's song.

About the author

Mandy is a poet and novelist based in Shropshire, England. She grew up in South Africa, learning about the land early on from her grandfather, the farmer and her father, the conservationist.

She loves the turning of the seasons, wild things, silence – and a good cup of tea.

This is her fifth collection of poetry. She has also written a novel under the pen name MJ Whyman.

Other works:

Poetry

Whispers from Southern Lands (2019)

Evidence (2019)

Fieldsong (2020)

Crow Dancing (2022)

Novel (MJ Whyman)

Like Water (2022)

Milton Keynes UK
Ingram Content Group UK Ltd.
UKHW020620300723
426013UK00009B/102

9 781739 133641